IMAGES OF
EGYPT

IMAGES OF
EGYPT

SIR MICHAEL WEIR

INTRODUCED BY
JAN MORRIS

PYRAMID BOOKS

Island of Gezira The branch of the Nile shown here separates the island of Gezira from the township of Giza, which now extends all the way to the pyramids. Gezira was given over to cultivation and royal parks until the late 19th century, when the British occupying authorities developed it with villas and gardens for officials and the exclusive playground of the Gezira Sporting Club. The island now boasts several modern hotels and a sumptuous opera house, the gift of Japan, which was opened in 1988. Across the other branch of the Nile the white mass of Cairo's first modern hotel, the Nile Hilton, stands on the site of the Qasr el-Nil barracks, familiar to generations of British troops and anathema to Egyptian nationalists.

First published in 1989
by Pyramid Books, an imprint of
The Hamlyn Publishing Group Limited
a division of The Octopus Publishing Group,
Michelin House, 81 Fulham Road, London SW3 6RB

ISBN 1-871-307848

Produced by Mandarin Offset
Printed and bound in Hong Kong

Introduction

can summon into mind at will my first impression of Egypt. It was encapsulated in a sensation which, four decades later, is still instantly accessible to me, and grows indeed richer in allusion every year.

I was on a ship sailing from Trieste, and when the buildings of the Egyptian coast were still only a vaporous smudge on the horizon, a kind of fragrance reached me. Its basis, I have since come to realize, was inadequately refined petroleum, but overlaid upon this oleaginous base was a host of lovelier scents both actual and imaginary. There were scents of dust and marshland, of sun-baked stone, of jasmine. There were scents of bright colours, as it were, scents that I associate in my mind with power and strangeness and extreme antiquity, and scents, I have to say, that still suggest to me squalor, sadness and a trace of fear.

Never was there a more complicated smell, even in the retroactive fancy; but then no country excites more complex responses than Egypt.

Not perhaps among Egyptians. Egyptians as a whole seem to me among the most straightforwardly patriotic people in the world, besides being the most anciently rooted, and their view of El Misr is generally unambiguous. It is the foreigner who is likely to be confused. Should we think of Egypt as an African country, or an Arab country? In Pharaonic images, or the images of Islam? As a Mediterranean, an Asian or an African Power? The currents cross in Egypt. It possesses sites sacred to Muslims, Christians, Jews and pagans, and if there is one plain symbolical frontier between the east and west of the world, it is the Suez Canal, cut through the Egyptian desert by European engineers. Napoleon called Egypt 'the most important country'; certainly it has a unique power to epitomize history and geography, and even to transcend time.

For instance, I have no difficulty in transferring myself all but physically back into the lost Levantine Egypt, the Egypt of foreign domination, in which I spent some of the formative years of my youth. I can still see the Greek cotton-brokers animated in their coffee-shops, the Jews and the Maltese, the British officers eating prawns at the Union Bar in what we used to call Alex. I can see the expatriate police officers in their tarbooshes, the British soldiers at their barrack windows, the polished French functionaries of the Suez Canal, the European ladies of leisure emerging from tea and sticky cakes at Groppi's tea-room to go shopping for silks and scents in Cairo's evening cool.

In reality that Egypt is utterly gone – all that is left is a trace of shabby alien grandeur, a boulevard here, a down-at-heel hotel along the corniche – yet the merest flick of a reminder can resurrect it for me. The dry preservative air does it, I think, keeping all Egyptian references sharp and vivid, and it is just as easy to send one's imagination back not just a couple of decades, but a few millennia into the still more absolutely extinct world of the Pharaohs. I was present years ago at the ceremonial opening of a Pharaonic tomb in Fayoum Province, believed to be that of a twelfth dynasty princess. Bands played, reporters, photographers and the Minister of Education were in attendance; but when the lid of the sarcophagus was opened, and found to contain nothing much but mud, I felt a genuine pang of sympathy for the poor lady whose fragile memory we were so vulgarly disturbing – almost as though, instead of living three thousand years before, she was actually a contemporary.

Of course the Pharaonic civilization immortalized itself deliberately in mighty monuments and meticulous works of art; but in a less tangible way too, like so much else in Egypt, it seems to have mastered the gift of *perpetual survival. Nothing could be much deader in the fact than the Pyramids of Giza, yet even among the degradations of tourism they remain a living presence in the suggestion; and there have been moments at Luxor, wandering through the ominous temple in the half-light, emerging bemused from the necropolitan Valley of the Kings, when I have felt the whole vanished society of the Pharaohs to be still all too potently in being, its kings and ministers watching the daily myriad of visitors as once they watched the daily labour of the slaves. No wonder so many people suppose themselves to be reincarnations of Ancient Egyptians.*

As for Islam, nowhere does its presence feel more ubiquitous than it does in Egypt – not in any fanatical or even intrusive way (most Egyptians are Sunnis of a particularly tolerant kind) but because here the faith has been ennobled into an inescapable component of everyday life, and a domestic fact. It is a universally accepted religion, but a social philosophy too. Cairo is the intellectual centre of Islam, the home of its oldest university and many of its most formidable thinkers; it is also a city where the simplest aspects of the creed impress all attitudes and affect all relationships.

No doubt this is partly the effect of the Muslim aesthetic, here to be experienced at its most comforting. The medieval mosques of Cairo are among the most exquisite assemblies of sacred buildings anywhere, and the crowded streets, markets, shops and tenements that jostle around them, constituting for so many centuries the central bazaar of the Islamic world, may be intolerably congested, unhygienic and even structurally unreliable, but are gloriously vivacious. More importantly, though, it is the frank and unquestioning acceptance of Islam by ordinary people that makes the faith so absolute in this country: the unpretentious pause in the day's bustle that follows the call to prayer, the guileless hospitality that Islam engenders, and the assurance of comradeship that springs from a profoundly shared conviction.

Binding all these ages and attitudes together, making a whole of them, sealing that half-abstract fragrance of mine, is something that I can only describe as Egyptness – the power of the country itself. The intellectual and artistic life of Egypt is concentrated nowadays in Cairo, the greatest city of Africa, hideously crowded, desperate with slums, but provided with nearly every concomitant of modernity – glitzy international hotels, an underground railway, high-rise buildings, the statutory tower with a revolving restaurant, an international airport and a large community of foreigners. Nevertheless most Egyptians, even now, live lives very close to the land, and are captive as they always have been, to the presence of that sine qua non *of Egyptian civilization, the river Nile.*

In many ways they are a terribly unlucky people, the fellahin or peasants of Egypt, condemned all too often to extreme poverty, denied all prospect of change or opportunity of improvement in a country that can scarcely keep up with its ever-multiplying population. They are squeezed into confined areas of fertility among the surrounding deserts, and despite all the achievements of modern engineering they are as dependent today as they ever were upon the bounty of the great river. But somehow in its rise and fall the Nile fertilizes their country spiritually as well as physically, and implants among the people, for all their deprivations, a sense of fatalistic serenity which itself seems part of the natural cycle.

It is a peasantry truly organic, with all that the adjective implies for better and for worse. The fellahin indulge in few excesses, of behaviour or of belief. Their humour is earthy, their pleasures are elemental. They appear to live to a rhythm as predictable and as fundamental as that of the river itself. Sometimes they suggest to me an allegorical people, their births and their deaths, their sorrows and their amusements, providing us with simple paradigms of existence itself.

No matter that, given half the chance, many of them would leave their simplicities for the chances of Cairo or the oil-rich Gulf: they are there, the Egyptians, by the river as they always have been, and if anything in this world is constant, there they will always remain.

I suppose it is really their judgement, not one's own, nor even that of the Cairo sophisticates, that should govern one's view of Egypt. It is theirs, after all, and to them it is the world, or at least the norm. They are at ease, figuratively and functionally, with the country they inhabit. It is an unmistakable country, they are an unmistakable people. The changeless beat of rural life, the bright colours and the river's muddy flow, an antique temple, perhaps, to be glimpsed at the desert's edge, the calm sounds and motions of Islam, the beckoning noise and merriment of city life, the rich tide of the Arabic language: perhaps when I myself think of Egypt as a congeries of smells, it is the nearest I can get in my own sensibility to the responses of simple Egyptians to their own country – beyond intellect or reason, that is, but inexpungible.

Jan Morris

The Step Pyramid at Saqqara Designed as the tomb of King Zoser, the founder of the 3rd Dynasty (2630 BC), this is the earliest stone-built structure in the world and a glorious monument not only to a powerful pharaoh but to his brilliant chief minister and architect, Imhotep. Earlier royal tombs had been built of mud-brick, reinforced with palm branches and reeds from the banks of the Nile nearby. As if to soften the break with tradition Imhotep built the stone pillars, doors and roofs of the pyramid temple complex in exact replica of those reed bundles and palm logs, which continue to serve a humble domestic function in Egyptian village life today.

The Pyramids of Giza Saqqara remained the necropolis of the ancient capital Memphis for the next three thousand years, and continues to yield fresh archaeological discoveries, while Memphis itself has disappeared beneath the villages and fields of the Nile. The fashion of building pyramid tombs reached its climax in the 4th and 5th Dynasties, with the massive pyramids of Giza. Though their smooth limestone facings have been stripped over the centuries for the building of Cairo, nothing can diminish the awe-inspiring sense of power they convey. The pyramid of Cheops comprised 2,300,000 blocks, each weighing two and a half tonnes. Its construction is not now believed to have required armies of slaves, but only small gangs of peasants released from agriculture during the flood season.

Aswan High Dam Eight hundred kilometres south of Giza the observation tower commemorates the completion of Egypt's 20th-century pyramid, the Aswan High Dam. It is dedicated to Soviet Egyptian friendship, which like the design went quickly out of fashion.

16

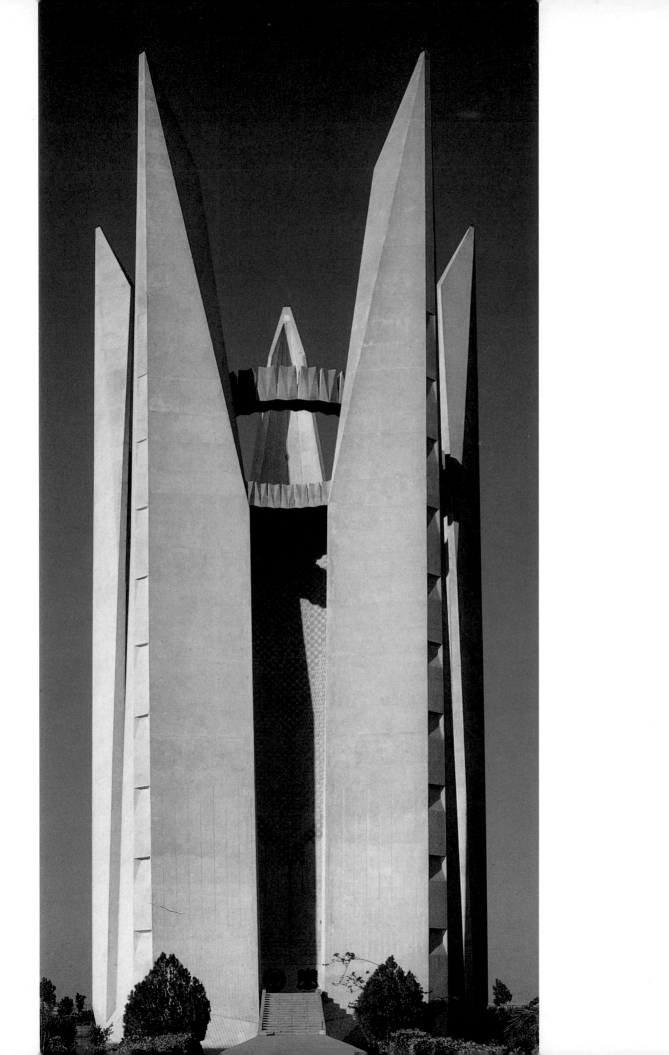

The Great Sphinx   Named by the Greeks
after their own – quite different – mytho-
logical monster, this was carved by the
builders of Chephren's pyramid from a
mound left by the quarrying of rock for the
Great Pyramid. With the body of a lion and
the head of the pharaoh, it stands guard
over the pyramid and has been a source of
mystery and wonder throughout the ages. A
tablet between its paws records how a
thousand years later Tuthmosis IV (1425
BC), in a youthful dream, heard the voice
of the Sphinx promise him the crown of all
Egypt if he would clear away the sand
which by then enveloped it. The Sphinx
now speaks with its own voice in sonorous
daily commentary for the *Son et Lumière* in
modern tourism.

Mosque of Ibn Tulun This is among the oldest and most celebrated mosques in the Islamic world. Ibn Tulun was sent to Cairo as governor by the Abbasid caliph in Baghdad in AD 868, but in time made Egypt into his own independent fief. He established a magnificent new quarter of palaces, which have all vanished, but the mosque survives in its original form. Its vast courtyard, covering some two and a half hectares, was designed to accommodate his several thousand followers at prayer-time. Today it stands out as an island of peace and calm in the middle of the congested modern city.

Mosque of Sulaiman Pasha This little 16th-century mosque, situated within the Citadel complex, is the earliest, and arguably the finest, mosque of the Ottoman period in Cairo. the main dome and its supporting arches are richly decorated in fresco with arabesques and Koranic descriptions.

Mosque of Mohamed Ali Almost a thousand years later Mohamed Ali, the last foreign conqueror of Egypt, who broke away from the Ottoman caliph and founded the dynasty that ended with King Farouk in 1952, built the mosque that bears his name. It is of little architectural merit but its domes and pencil-slim minarets make a striking silhouette on the skyline above the sprawl of Cairo. Mohamed Ali sited his mosque within the citadel that the 12th-century monarch Saladin had built above the city as a defence against the Crusaders, largely with the labour of Crusader captives. It was also within these walls that Mohamed Ali entertained the princes of the old 'Mameluke' regime before massacring them to consolidate his coup.

Thebes Some 700 kilometres south of Cairo the modern village of Luxor marks the site of ancient Thebes, and the grandest complex of pharaonic temples and tombs in Egypt. Thebes first came to prominence in the Middle Kingdom (*c.*2000 BC) when its rulers re-united Upper and Lower Egypt into a single empire. It was they who introduced the worship of the sun-god Amun-Re, later the principal deity of Egypt. In the New Kingdom (1570–1080 BC) Thebes emerged as the centre of a brilliant renaissance of art and architecture, sustained by booty and tribute from all over Asia and Africa. The living city, with its priests, administrators and merchants, grew up on the east bank of the Nile, while the west bank, as the place of the setting sun, was reserved for the dead and their monuments.

Below Beyond the Sacred Lake is the huge temple complex of Karnak, covering a total of 25 hectares.

The Avenue of Rams, Karnak An avenue of sphinxes with the head of a ram – the symbol of the god Amun – leads to the Great Hall of Columns. They originally flanked the whole length of the sacred road between the temples at Karnak and Luxor, a distance of nearly three kilometres. The greater part of the avenue lies underneath the present-day village, but it has been excavated where it approaches the Luxor temple to reveal two imposing rows of sphinxes with human heads (*see overleaf*).

Temple of Luxor The temple itself, like that at Karnak, is entered between two huge pylons, or massive backward-sloping towers which resemble protective ramparts as much as sanctuary walls. In front stand six colossal statues of Ramses II, probably the most famous of all Egyptian pharaohs, who ruled for 66 years in the 13th century BC and left innumerable monuments in stone, mostly in his own image. He was not above erasing his predecessors' names from their monuments and substituting his own, as at Luxor where he claims credit for building the handsome colonnaded temple adjoining his; it had in fact been erected by Amenophis III a hundred years before and continued by Tutankhamun.

Temple of Amenophis III The elegant columns of this temple have capitals in the form of a cluster of papyrus buds. The obelisk is one of two erected in front of the pylons by Ramses II; the other was removed in 1836 to adorn the Place de la Concorde in Paris. This part of the temple was later converted to various other uses, including a shrine for Alexander the Great and an early Christian church. It is only in recent years that the Luxor complex has been uncovered from beneath the debris of centuries, so that the names inscribed by Napoleon's officers and other early travellers are now just discernible at the top of tall columns, which were then at ground level. In a mansion built on this site the Englishwoman Lucie Duff Gordon lived for seven years in the 1860s, in search of better health, and wrote the celebrated letters home that give a sensitive picture of ordinary life in Egypt at that time.

The Colossi of Memnon   The greatest
festival of Thebes in its heyday centred on
the procession of the god Amun by river-
boat from Karnak to Luxor, and scenes
from this festival are depicted in vivid relief
on the walls of the Luxor temple. The god
also made regular ceremonial visits to the
tomb temples on the west bank. Then as
now, the first sight to greet the visitor was
the twin statues of Amenophis III, which
the Romans mistakenly christened the Colossi of Memnon. They stand in flat fields,
looking somewhat forlorn and incongruous
as well as faceless, but they originally
marked the entrance to the pharaoh's vast
funerary temple – which barely a century
later became a stone quarry for his
successors.

Tutankhamun's tomb The walls of the burial chamber are decorated with scenes from the Book of the Dead, depicting the pharoah's reception into the afterlife.

Temple of Horus, Edfu The cult of Hathor at Dendera was closely connected with that of the god Horus at Edfu, south of Luxor. The link was celebrated in an annual river festival in which the goddess Hathor sailed upstream to Edfu, where she went through a marriage ceremony with Horus. It was clearly an occasion for merry-making, as related in the temple texts: 'Wine flows like the inundation of the Nile; myrrh and incense can be smelt a mile away . . . the king's party is in its full regalia; the young people are drunk; the young girls are beautiful to see; jollity is all around . . . there is no sleep till dawn.'

The Edfu temple, with its huge pylons, colonnades and pillared halls modelled on Karnak, took 180 years to build and is the best preserved of all Egyptian temples. The fine granite statue of Horus, the falcon-god, stands guard at the entrance of the pylons wearing the double crown of Upper and Lower Egypt.

Horus and Hathor Wearing the double crown in a relief at Edfu, Horus looks across at his bride Hathor, whose cow-eared image crowns the lotus-cluster capitals at her temple at Dendera.

Edfu temple, like most of those in Upper Egypt, was later used as a church by the early Christians.

Frieze from the temple at Kom Ombo The left-hand figure is probably the crocodile god Suchos, who was especially revered at this Ptolemaic temple on the Nile north of Aswan. Numerous mummified crocodiles were found at this site and may still be seen there. On the right is the god Horus wearing the double crown. Both figures have been badly defaced by the chisels of early Christian occupants of the temple, who made a habit of obliterating the features of Pharaonic deities.

Hieroglyphic inscriptions   The hieroglyphic script came to Egypt, probably from Mesopotamia, about 3100 BC and remained in use until the end of the 4th century AD. The symbols, numbering nearly 700, are not an alphabet; they can represent either the object they portray or a single letter. They defied decipherment until the discovery of the Rosetta Stone by Napoleon's troops in 1799 provided the key in the form of parallel hieroglyphic and Greek texts. In these examples the symbols of the sedge and the bee represent Upper and Lower Egypt, while the seated figure is a pharaoh holding the crook and flail signifying royal authority.

Temples of Philae   The temple complex on the little island of Philae near Aswan, constructed in the Graeco-Roman period and dedicated to the goddess Isis, is indisputably the most beautiful of the ancient sites in Egypt. In its heyday the Isis cult gave the island a reputation for magic and mystery that attracted pilgrims long after Christianity had become the official national religion. Later on the abandoned temples, surrounded by trees and undergrowth, had a particular romantic appeal for the Victorians who christened Philae the 'Pearl of Egypt'. In the 20th century, however, the temples were covered for most of the year by the Nile waters stored above the original Aswan Dam, while the building of the High Aswan dam would have submerged them for ever. They were saved by a huge engineering operation funded by UNESCO, whereby the buildings were dismantled and re-erected stone by stone on a neighbouring island above the new water level.

Abu Simbel The colossal statues of Ramses II at Abu Simbel might be called the apotheosis of that great monarch's self-aggrandisement. Carved out of the living rock on the west bank of the Nile some 300 kilometres south of Aswan, they form the entrance facade, 32 metres high, to a great temple within the rock dedicated to the two principal gods and to Ramses himself. The statues between the legs of the colossi represent – on what Ramses no doubt considered an appropriate scale – his mother and his favourite wife. Within the temple, the walls are covered from floor to roof with reliefs chronicling the pharaoh's military triumphs, including unusually life-like scenes ranging from the interrogation of Hittite spies to supper in the sergeants' mess.

Abu Simbel reached the height of its international fame in the 1960s thanks to the UNESCO engineering project to save it, like Philae in the 1970s, from the rising waters of Lake Nasser. Sliced into over a thousand blocks, the whole temple was reassembled on higher ground in a position indistinguishable from the original, but supported from behind by an artificial mountain constructed over a concrete frame.

Mosque of Ibn Tulun, Cairo Ahmed ibn Tulun modelled his mosque on the Great Mosque of Samarra in Iraq, where he himself grew up. It is built of brick and surrounded by a double wall, the space between which served – as it still does – to shelter the worshippers from the hustle and bustle of the dwellings and markets outside. The central structure is an ablutions fountain, added in AD 1296. The minaret with its unusual external spiral staircase, is an exact copy of the minaret at Samarra. The delicate crenellations that decorate the parapet are unique to this mosque, and the pointed arches were used here for the first time in Muslim architecture. They pre-date the Western Gothic arch by two centuries.

Mosque of Sultan Hassan, Cairo Not far from Ibn Tulun is the great mosque of Sultan Hassan, who reigned in the middle of the 14th century. It has a grandeur rivalling that of Ibn Tulun, but it presents a more forbidding appearance with its massive external walls and towering entrance – the tallest in the Islamic world. The spacious courtyard, with ablutions fountain in the centre, has four immense arched recesses in its walls in which the students of the Koran used to sit at the feet of their shaikhs. The arch leading to the sanctuary, from which the lamps depend, is the biggest such structure in Cairo.

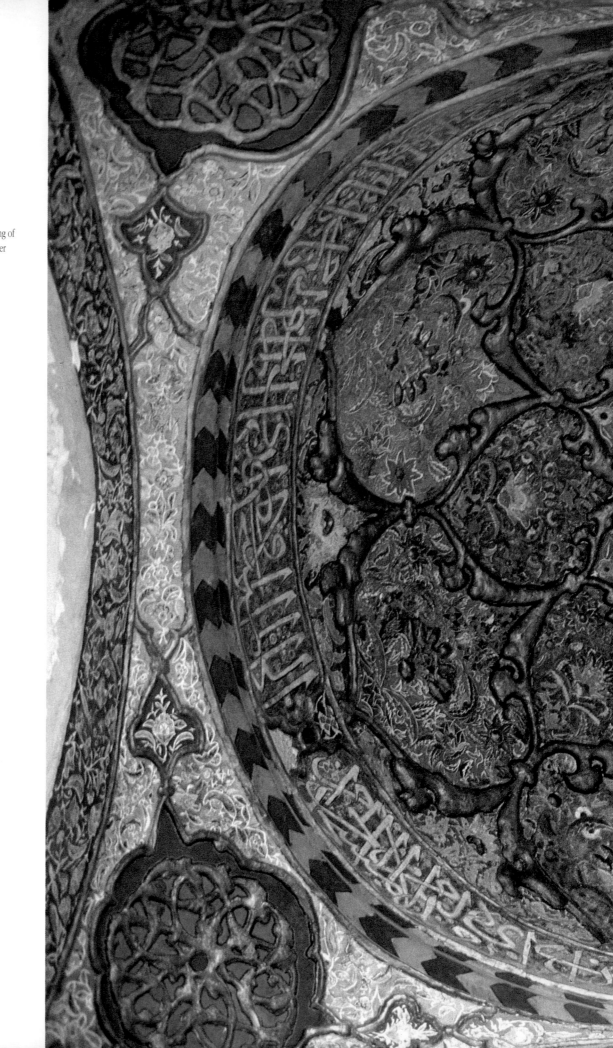

Mosque of Sulaiman Pasha The ceiling of the main dome of the mosque, the lower part of which is shown on page 20.

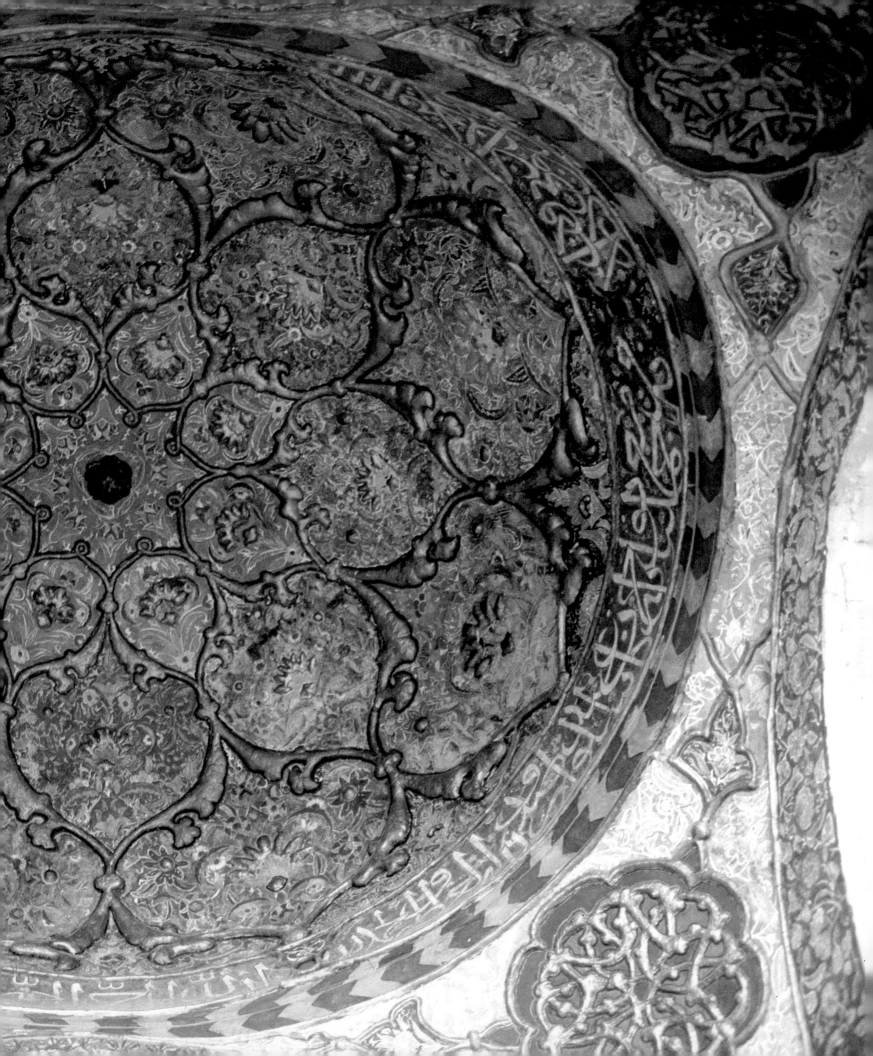

Mosque of Al Azhar, Cairo Founded in AD 970 by the first ruler of the Fatimid dynasty, this mosque has been the foremost teaching centre of Sunni Islam for the past 800 years, and has a good claim to be the oldest university in the world. Students come to Al Azhar from all over the Muslim world, and are constantly to be seen in the courtyard praying, reciting or memorizing the Koran. The university has meanwhile expanded to include modern faculties like medicine, science and languages. The building is the finest Fatimid monument in Egypt. Its keel-shaped arches are supported on a variety of columns taken from earlier Christian buildings, and surmounted by saw-toothed crenallations not previously seen in Cairo.

Musafirkhana Palace, Cairo Built by a rich merchant in the 18th century, the palace was later appropriated by the royal family, and the notorious Khedive Ismail was born there in 1830. The mashrabiya screens on the upper floor are a good example of the arrangement for the womenfolk in all such Muslim households. Impenetrable from the outside, mashrabiya (lattice-work) allowed the ladies inside to observe what was going on in the central courtyard of the house without being seen themselves.

Mosque of Al Azhar, Cairo The wooden projection is a lecture pulpit in traditional mashrabiya style, while behind it rises the principal minaret, an elaborate 15th-century structure, over the main entrance to the mosque.

Mosque of Aqsunqar, Cairo   The mosque of Aqsunqar is named after a son-in-law of the famous Mameluk sultan Al Nasir Muhamad (see pages 72–73), and dates from the mid-14th century. Situated half-way down the medieval street that connects the Citadel with the walled Fatimid city, it is popularly known as the blue mosque on account of the blue tiles which were added three centuries later. With its colonnade and well planted courtyard the mosque offers a quiet and colourful refuge from the dusty streets.

Madrasa of Al-Nasir Muhamad, Cairo
This Gothic-style doorway to an Islamic school not only looks like a church door, it is one, and was brought from a Crusader church at Acre which the founder's brother had captured in 1291. The builder was Al-Nasir Muhamad, one of the early Mameluke sultans who ruled throughout the first half of the 13th century. His reign is generally regarded as the golden age of medieval Egypt, before its long decline. His family were active patrons of the arts and spent lavishly on mosques, schools, hospitals and other public buildings, many of which survive as monuments not only to their creators but to their good taste.

Baramous Monastery, Wadi Natrun The Coptic Church ('Copt' comes from the Greek word for Egypt) traces its origins to the mission and martyrdom of St Mark in Alexandria, and claims to be the oldest church in the world. It was the 4th-century Egyptian St Antony who, by the example of his hermit's life, established monasticism as a mass movement which in less than 200 years spread as far as Ireland and northern Europe. Most of the Egyptian monasteries were abandoned long ago, but four of the most famous survived, in the Wadi Natrun desert north of Cairo. Baramous, shown here, was founded in the 4th century.

St Antony's Monastery This is situated in barren mountainous country west of Cairo, at the reputed site of the hermit's cave. The church shown here is modern, but there are others within the walls dating back to the 13th century. The gardens, fed by three springs, cover some two and a half hectares and contain citrus fruits and a vineyard as well as palm·trees, which make a welcome splash of colour against the arid landscape. Although the Copts now comprise only about 12 per cent of Egypt's population, the past 15 years have witnessed a remarkable religious revival among Egyptian Christians, in which many men have abandoned professional careers for the monasteries.

Old Cairo The most demonstrably ancient relics of Coptic history are to be found in Old Cairo, where the so-called Hanging Church was built directly above the main gate of the Roman city, then known as Babylon. The church of St Sergius nearby claims to have given shelter in its crypt to the Holy Family during the flight to Egypt. The ancient garden doorway is in a street adjoining the church.

Sun, river and desert could be said to epitomize the essence of Egyptian life throughout the ages. The ancient Egyptians worshipped the sun-god Re as the giver of life, reborn each morning from the womb of the sky-goddess Nut and swallowed again by her each evening. The cycle of the river Nile, bringing the annual inundation that restored life to the fields, was an equally important influence on Egyptian thought; it probably accounts for the stability of Egyptian society throughout history. The desert on the other hand is seen by most Egyptians as alien and hostile, devoid of the romance that Europeans tend to find in it. The dunes are a familiar landmark just beyond Cairo airport.

The Suez Canal The Canal mirrors the political history of Egypt. Just as earlier projects, from the pharaohs onwards, to link the Red Sea with the Mediterranean via the Nile were abandoned for fear of attracting foreign intervention, the Canal – completed in 1869 – brought much trouble and little benefit to Egypt in its first hundred years. Now it is enlarged to many times its original size and capable of taking all but the largest supertankers, a major revenue-earner and perhaps the most sophisticated and efficient operation in the country.

War in the desert   The deserts of Egypt offer poignant reminders of the role they have played as battlefields throughout history. The battles of the western desert are commemorated by three monuments erected by the major combatants, each in distinctive national style. The Commonwealth cemetery at El Alamein stands on the ridge from which the Allied forces launched their final offensive in October 1942, looking southward over the desert. On the walls of the cloister are inscribed the names of the 11,945 Commonwealth nationals who fell in the desert campaigns.

In the stony deserts of Sinai in the east the forlorn remains of vehicles destroyed in the 1973 war with Israel can still be found. Largely demilitarized now, and guarded by the MFO (Multinational Force and Observers), Sinai is being developed for a more peaceful future.

Sinai A short distance inland from the Gulf of Suez, which with its oilwells is the main source of Egypt's oil production, stretch the forbidding mountain ranges of central and south Sinai. Extensive traces still remain of the turquoise, copper and other mines worked here in ancient times, together with the ruins of pharaonic temples and rock inscriptions in hieroglyphs. Other inscriptions from later periods – in Nabatean, Greek, Latin and Arabic – abound in the tracks that cross the peninsula and testify to its historical importance as a route for trade, pilgrimage and war.

The White Desert Some 300 kilometres west of the Nile, well south of the western desert as usually defined, is one of the most extraordinary desert landscapes of Egypt. Formed largely of outcrops of gypsum on a gravel plain, the overall effect is of a blindingly white snowfield with polar ice-floes and frozen waves. Virtually the only vegetation in this region exists in a chain of four oases that run in a crescent from due west of Cairo to west of Aswan. The white desert lies between the oases of Bahariya and Farafra.

Life in the desert The oases of Sinai are smaller but the desert between them is less inhospitable. Here a little girl draws water by pump from a well on the dividing line – which in Egypt is invariably clear-cut – between the desert and the sown. On the right a bedu boy shelters from the sun under the ubiquitous acacia tree, almost the only form of shade the desert offers.

St Catherine's Monastery   St Catherine's monastery in southern Sinai belongs to a different tradition from Egypt's other monasteries. By the 4th century AD the mountain of Jebel Musa (Moses' mountain) had become identified with the site of the burning bush of Exodus and was attracting hermits and pilgrims. The monastery was founded from Byzantium by the emperor Justinian in AD 537, both as a settlement for the monks and as a garrison against invaders. The foundation never had any connection with the Coptic church, which had broken away from Byzantium by the 4th century, and it remains separate to this day. The monks are Greek and belong to the Greek Orthodox church.

The windlass was used in times of danger to haul up supplies, and men, through the wooden hatch visible high up on the outside walls.

St Catherine's Monastery St Catherine's was largely spared from pillage by the successive armies that passed that way. According to tradition the monks obtained a letter of immunity from the prophet Muhamad that protected them during the later Arab conquests. Thus the extant buildings reflect all periods from Justinian onwards. The main church, with massive doors carved from cedars of Lebanon, dates from the early period. The foliage in the foreground is said to be the original burning bush that has miraculously re-newed itself down the ages. The other buildings include a mosque, provided in the 13th century for neighbouring Muslims, with whom the monks have always kept on the best of terms. (They may have greater difficulty adjusting to the latest addition to their environment: the construction of a tourist village just below the monastery.)

St Paul's Monastery At the summit of Jebel Musa the monks have constructed a simple chapel. The ascent, long but not difficult, provides a breathtaking view over the jagged peaks of the Sinai range, especially at sunrise.

The fresco comes from the Coptic monastery of St Paul the Theban on the west coast of the Gulf of Suez. It marks the site of the cave in which Paul reputedly dwelt for nearly a hundred years, and to which St Antony, who was almost equally aged, walked from the other side of the mountain to bury him. The monastery is more isolated than St Antony's, but hardly less popular with pilgrims and other visitors.

Cairo   Egypt experienced an extraordinary surge in economic growth in the
years after the 1973 war, thanks largely to
President Sadat's 'open door' policy for
foreign investment. One effect was an
explosion of building in Cairo, for international hotels and luxury accommodation.
It not only transformed the appearance of
the city into a Mediterranean Manhattan but
caused major problems for traffic and
public utilities. Alongside these symbols of
affluence, in stark contrast, stand the
densely packed and overcrowded dwellings
of the poor, who continue to be attracted
from the country to the capital in numbers
greater than a valiant low-cost house-
building programme can cope with.

Central Cairo The focus of this scene, *right*, could be described as the living heart of Cairo, for both the ordinary Cairene and the ordinary tourist. The minaret of Al Azhar in the foreground looks across al Azhar street to the maidan (square) of the Sayyidna Hussein mosque with its slender minaret. This 19th-century mosque, though dedicated to the 7th- century Shi'a martyr Hussein, has become the centre for the principal Sunni festivals of Cairo. Especially during the holy month of Ramadan, the mosque and the square are filled at night with good-humoured crowds celebrating the feast and watching a variety of side-shows.

Khan el Khalili, Cairo The Khan, or caravanserai market, was established in the 14th century as a forum for foreign traders, but now specializes in traditional Egyptian crafts. Every conceivable trade is represented in its narrow streets, each within its own quarter – goldsmiths, silversmiths, coppersmiths, metalworkers, tentmakers, glassblowers, dyers, perfumiers, carpetmakers and woodcarvers.

Camel Market, Imbaba There are many aspects of traditional life in Cairo that continue completely unaffected by the trappings of the modern metropolis and unseen by the casual visitor. One such is the camel market at Imbaba, an ancient and unmodernized quarter of the city, where herds of camels converge from the deserts once a week to be sold for butcher meat, a prized delicacy when dried and cured.

Khan el Khalili, Cairo

Cairo The residents in this block of flats
are fortunate compared with the bulk of
Cairo's population. But the washing lines
testify to the lack of open space that is one
of the greatest problems of this teeming
city.

Modern Cairo A section of a street in central Cairo reflects both present and past. A cinema of unmistakably 1930s vintage advertises a torrid-looking but undoubtedly respectable film *Call this love*. Shops on either side feature 'gentlemen's fashions' and Brazilian coffee, while the snack-bar in between is named after Kleber, the general whom Napoleon left in charge when he fled from Egypt in 1800, and who was assassinated by the mob. Farther along the street stands the imposing principal synagogue of Cairo, closed since the departure of the Jewish community after the revolution.

Selling liquorice water The street vendor of drinks of all kinds, tea, karkady (crushed hibiscus petals), liquorice water or simply water, is a ubiquitous sight in the main towns during the summer, carrying his patent dispenser specially manufactured in the Khan el Khalili.

Upper Egypt Fresco painting on the walls of stuccoed or mud-brick houses is a favourite form of domestic art in Egypt, especially in the south. The basic theme is invariably religious, featuring a portrayal of the Kaaba shrine at Mecca, designed to show that the house-owner has performed the Hajj, or pilgrimage. For the rest the artist gives free rein to imagination, although even apparently secular scenes like these are suggestive of Omar Khayyam and the prospective delights of paradise.

Village street   The village houses above,
alongside an irrigation canal in Middle
Egypt, show the universal form of construction in which roofs are seldom
completed but equipped with the rudi-
ments of another storey in case of need.
Rain, being minimal except on the Mediterranean, is not a problem. Other houses
may be topped by a dovecot, a feature
common to every Egyptian village; the function of the pigeons is to provide fertilizer
rather than meat.

Farming This agricultural scene is typical of thousands of small-holdings in the Delta. Although the Aswan High dam now provides year-round irrigation, permitting up to three crops a year, population growth, together with post-revolutionary policies of industrialization, has meant that Egypt, like so many developing countries, is no longer self-sufficient in food production.

Egypt is now the world's largest importer of wheat after the Soviet Union and China, and has the highest per capita consumption. The most popular crop, as shown here, is bersim or alfalfa, grown as fodder for cattle to satisfy the growing demand for meat, in a country where not long ago the staple diet was the black bean.

Aswan The nature of the produce – dried dates in numerous varieties, ground nuts, dried hibiscus petals and dried herbs – as well as recumbent shopkeeper reflect the heat and dryness of Upper Egypt at Aswan.

Canal, Upper Egypt Despite the hi-tech of the Aswan Dam and computerized control of the Nile flow, irrigation methods are still, at grass roots level, largely the same as those of two thousand years ago. The Archimedes screw *above* raises water from one level, such as the main irrigation canal *right*, to another by the simple means of a spiral of grooves turned by hand, and has the great merit of being portable. As its name implies, it was introduced into Egypt by its Greek inventors during the Ptolemaic period.

The Suez Canal at Ismailia The old Suez Canal Company hospital is seen from the opposite bank of the canal from that shown on pp. 80–81. The mosque and minaret are modern. The stone-built revetment is new too, and was constructed to consolidate the banks of the canal, along most of its length, as part of the major widening operation of the late 1970s.

Egypt's largest oasis A somewhat more familiar contraption than those pictured earlier is found in the Fayoum, the huge cultivated area 80 kilometres west of Cairo which is sometimes described as Egypt's largest oasis. Its water is in fact supplied from the Nile by a long canal dug in pharaonic times, the Bahr Yusuf. It was the Greek ex-soldiers from Alexander's armies and others who settled in the Fayoum from the 3rd century BC who greatly developed its agriculture by land reclamation, and by irrigation devices like these massive wooden water wheels reminiscent of those used later in European mills.

Water wheel The irrigation machine known as a *dolab* performs the same function as the Archimedes screw in greater volume but is turned by an ox, a donkey, water-buffalo or even camel, walking blind-folded in a perpetual circle. The wheel turned by the animal is connected by wooden cogs to a large pulley wheel which turns an endless chain of water-pots; these pick up the water from below and dis-charge it at the top of their cycle into the irrigation channel.

Carrying sugar cane A camel carries a load of sugar cane in Upper Egypt. The shuttered villa beyond will have been built in the 19th century by a landowner, or pasha, when the cultivation of sugar cane was introduced on a commercial scale. Since the land reforms that followed the 1952 revolution it might well have been taken over by peasants like the owner of the camel.

Village at Luxor More mural artistry, with signs of inspiration both ancient and modern. Between the name of the pharaoh Sennufer above and the frieze of lotus and papyrus plants below the owner advertises his workshop of alabaster wares. This is the village of Gurna, on the west bank opposite Luxor. Situated alongside the Valley of the Kings, and literally on top of the Tombs of the Nobles, the village comprises a close community which has made its livelihood from the necropolis – whether tomb preparation, tomb robbing, or the manufacture and supply of antiques to the tourist trade – since the time when the first pharaohs were buried here.

Christian village This village is far from typical, and will be as unfamiliar to Egyptian as to foreign eyes. The domed structures in the background are the tombs of Christian villagers, and are found in other Christian cemeteries in middle Egypt near the principal Christian cities of Minya and Assiut. What is unusual about this village, situated near the east bank of the Nile in Middle Egypt, is that identical domed buildings, as shown in the photograph, are inhabited by the living alongside those of their ancestors.

Desert dwellers Both these scenes
feature desert dwellers, but there is a world
of difference between them. The vegetable
market is in the large oasis of Kharga, 300
kilometres to the west of Luxor, which has
been a town since pharaonic times. It was
the centre of Nasser's ambitious New Valley
agricultural project, scaled down when the
underground water proved insufficient. The
veiled girls belong to a tribe of beduin
whose home is the stony desert of western
Sinai. There both water and soil are at a
premium and will never offer an alternative
to the nomadic way of life. The rocks in the
vicinity are covered with Nabatean
inscriptions, though here they are
obscured by later graffiti in Arabic.

Sinai A bedouin girl leads her donkey to collect water from the well.

Cairo Goatherd and shepherd boy await customers in the market at Imbaba.

Aswan market Woven reed baskets, crude but sturdy, are the universal means of transport, usually on donkey-back, of every conceivable material from cabbages to cement.

Upper Egypt A cheerful washing-day scene, for cooking pots and clothes, on a canal bank in Upper Egypt.

Aswan market This type of basket-work *above*, though aimed chiefly at the tourist market, is a traditional Nubian craft and combines fine weaving with pleasing colour and design.

Luxor Waiting for a fare outside the Winter Palace hotel in Luxor. The hotel – and quite possibly the carriage – was built to accommodate the annual influx of wealthy Europeans who established the fashion of wintering in Upper Egypt in the period up to the First World War. The attractions of climate and antiquities remain unchanged, but the number of visitors has multiplied, while the building of hotels and cruise ships to accommodate them struggles to keep pace.

Camel trek A herd of camels arrives at the oasis of Bahariya on its way to the camel market and the abattoirs of Cairo. They have been driven north from the Sudan, over an ancient route known as the Forty Day Road, which follows the crescent of oases in Nubia and the western desert. The camel was not introduced into Africa until the Roman period, but for centuries thereafter was the essential vehicle for the slave trade, and pilgrim traffic, that crossed the deserts between Libya and central Africa and the Red Sea, usually in conditions of extreme hardship and danger.

Oasis of Bahariya Mud-brick dwelling and garden wall in Bahariya. The orchards at Bahariya, fed by abundant springs, are among the most prolific in Egypt, producing citrus fruits, dates, apricots and olives. The walls protect the crops from the wind and wind-blown sand; it is a never-ending struggle to keep the shifting sands at bay.

The River Nile Returning to the Nile, the felucca, with its traditional lateen rig, is a graceful and versatile craft for both passengers and freight. Its importance increased when the proliferation of dams and road/rail bridges in the 19th century restricted the passage of larger vessels up the Nile delta to Cairo and beyond.

Aswan   The town of Aswan stands at the historic frontier between Egypt and Nubia, just below the First Cataract where the Nile flows over a wide barrier of jumbled rocks before resuming its placid progress to the sea. Thus Aswan's historical role has been that of garrison town, and minor entrepot for traffic between Egypt and the Sudan. It acquired greater commercial importance when the sugar cane industry was developed in the 19th century, and the High Dam brought hydro-electric power plants in the 20th.

Yet it retains the general appearance of a tranquil backwater, not without archaeological interest but no rival to Luxor, and attractive chiefly for its hot dry climate and the verdant islands in the broad expanse of Nile. The view here is from the west bank. The villa of the Begum Agha Khan is in the foreground, Kitchener's island on the left, and Elephantine island beyond, with its unsightly modern hotel at one end and archaeological excavations at the other.

Aswan The houseboat seen here is a modest descendant of the grander house-boats, or 'dhahabiyas', which the affluent Victorian visitor would hire to cruise the Upper Nile. Later, more sumptuous, versions were berthed along the banks of the Nile in Cairo as permanent accommo-dation until fairly recent years. The past decade has witnessed a steady increase in the number and especially size of commer-cial cruise ships ferrying tourists between the riverine sites, to the point where there is a distinct problem of congestion. Tourist feluccas, on the other hand, serve to enhance the landscape at Aswan, as they discharge their cargo on to the west bank for a visit to the tomb of the Agha Khan, seen on the skyline.

Selling beads A man carries his wares over one shoulder in the tourist market.

Aswan A Nubian oarsman rows his felucca-load of tourists across the Nile.

Over By sunset the west bank will once again be left to the disk of Amun-Re, presiding over the spirits of the countless generations who made it their last resting place.

Index

Picture Acknowledgements

All photographs by DAVID TUNNICLIFFE with the exception of the following:

Charles Fowkes 30–1, 76, 98, 131, 135; Robert Harding Picture Library 1, 2; Hutchinson Picture Library 14, 129,/Bernard Regent 4–5; Robert O'Dea 18, 24–5, 26, 27, 28–9, 32, 33, 34–5, 40–1, 41, 42, 43, 45, 46 left, 47, 48, 49, 50–1, 52, 58, 59, 62, 97, 100, 102–3, 104, 106–7, 120, 128, 130, 134; Spectrum Colour Library 38, 39, 117, 118, 119; Stuart Windsor 6, 19, 53, 54 top, 54 bottom, 55, 63, 70, 96, 104–5, 109, 136, 137, 139, 140, 141, 142–3

Series editor: Alison Leach